bewitching CHARMS FOR HEALTH, WEALTH & HAPPINESS

bewitching
CHARMS FOR HEALTH, WEALTH & HAPPINESS

RAVEN TEMPEST

First published in Great Britain in 2003 by Cassell Illustrated, a division of
Octopus Publishing Group Limited, 2-4 Heron Quays, London E14 4JP

A CIP catalogue record for this book is available from the British Library.

Distributed in the United States of America by Sterling Publishing Co.
Inc., 387 Park Avenue South, New York, NY 10016-8810

Essential oils and other remedies as recommended in the charms and
spells should be used with care as some may be unsuitable for use with
particular medical and health conditions such as pregnancy. This book
should not be considered as a medical manual and replacement for
professional medical treatment where necessary. A medical practitioner
should be consulted in all matters related to health, and it is recommended
that you seek professional advice if you suspect that you have a medical
problem. While the advice and information contained in this book is
believed to be accurate, neither the author nor the publisher can accept
any legal responsibility for any illness or injury sustained whilst following
any of the suggestions made herein.

ISBN 1 84403 088 1

Printed in China.

CONTENTS

INTRODUCTION

The three concepts of health, wealth and happiness
are intrinsically linked, and in this book I will provide
advice in the form of rituals and spells that will help
you to achieve all three.

Naturally, good physical health is a key factor to
how we feel generally, and stress and tensions, born
out of frustration of our desires, can aggravate the
body and affect morale. We can help to prevent
physical ailments by looking into our souls and
identifying our emotional and spiritual needs, and

nurturing them. Understanding one's own emotions is an integral part of the process of healing, and achieving balance and harmony within ourselves will enable us to reach our full potential, both professionally and personally.

Whilst money and wealth should not be the sole focus in life, or used as the only measure of success, I disagree with the concept that to achieve spiritual fulfilment one needs to be poor. Success at work and a healthy bank balance reduce the everyday stresses

continued over...

INTRODUCTION continued

around us, and allow us to focus on our biological
and emotional needs in a harmonious environment.
Similarly, one of the biggest hurdles that prevents us
from being socially and professionally rich and
successful is the mental barrier of negativity and
doubt. By removing obstacles and adopting a positive
approach we reinforce the message that we deserve
the finer things in life. Using this book, you can find a
balance between your material and spiritual needs,
and have a happy and healthy lifestyle.

I have created a mixture of powerful and uplifting rituals taken from Eastern and Western spiritual cultures to guide you through the practical steps to healing and help you to turn your dreams into reality. Through the incorporation of symbols and powerful colours into the rituals, you can transform all aspects of your life, and open the doors to good fortune, success and spiritual fulfilment.

Raven Tempest

TRANSFORMING A WISH
INTO A SPELL

A wish is the seed of a spell and the expression 'you reap what you sow' definitely applies in this case. It is not enough just to hope or fantasize about your personal desires. To turn dreams into reality, you have to transform your wish into a spell but, even then, you need to ensure a successful outcome by the actions you take. For example, if you were to cast a spell to lose weight, it would only work if you took the necessary actions to complement the spell. If you carried on eating too much, or the wrong type of food, and did not bother to exercise, then the spell would almost certainly fail. The same principle applies if you were to cast a spell to bring you instant riches. The spell would not work if you just sat at home anticipating the arrival of cash.

The idea is that magical spells work in conjunction with the down-to-earth actions that we need to take in order to create opportunities and open the doors to success. It is up to us to take up the challenge and help ourselves.

COMPOSING THE SPELL

Once you have decided on the spell, the next stage is to compose it. This is a good way to ensure that your spell reflects your true wishes and that you have covered all possible loopholes. There are two ways to compose a spell: you can either write it down or say it out loud – or you can do both. Writing a spell has the advantage of giving you the opportunity to change your mind and reword it if you so wish. Always remember to ask for your spell to happen in the right way, and for it not to cause harm to you or anyone else. By incorporating these words into your spell, you are safeguarding the outcome from any adverse reactions, such as the spell working only as a result of misfortune.

A mistake people sometimes make is to worry about the route their spell should take in order for it to be successful. Please leave the small details to the divine powers – they are the best judges. Remember, the sky is the limit, so do not restrict yourself; the pot of gold at the end of the rainbow is well within your grasp.

Creating spells is great fun and, once you have perfected the art, you can begin to create your own. However, before you do so, please make sure that you have read this chapter thoroughly because it is important to know what you are doing, especially when it involves your safety and the safety of others.

DOS AND DON'TS OF MAGIC

DO be careful what you wish for and of the wording of the spell you create and cast. You will get whatever you have asked for, but perhaps not in the way you expected. For example, money could arrive as compensation for an accident, or even a death.

DO always ask for the spell to happen in an appropriate way and that it shall not cause harm to you or anyone else.

DO cast all spells within a pentacle circle of protection and whilst you are in the alpha state (pages 14–19).

DO ask for your magic to work for the good of all.

DO take your time with each spell, carefully thinking it through and considering the consequences of your projections.

DO persevere if your magic does not work. It could be that what you have asked for may not have been for the good of all. Therefore, rethink your spell and try again.

DON'T ever use magic to cause harm or as a weapon to threaten people. Your action and thoughts will come back to you threefold.

DON'T be flippant when you are casting spells. Think carefully about what you are saying and what you project. Use your intuition as well as your intellect.

DON'T cast spells with children or pets in the same room.

DON'T overdo magic. If you cast too many spells in a month you will burn out your magical energy.

DON'T cast spells during an eclipse because the moon will unfavourably affect the outcome.

DON'T doubt your own magical powers as this will weaken your spell.

DON'T discuss your spells once they are released.

THE MAGIC FORMULA
Spell-casting ritual

I will now guide you step by step through the process of shifting levels of consciousness, forming a pentacle circle of protection, and casting and releasing your spell.

1. Shifting consciousness

Sit in front of your altar or in your sacred area and slowly close your eyes, relaxing your mind and body. Once you feel sufficiently relaxed, start counting down from fourteen to one.

As you count, you may experience a tingling sensation. This is your brainwave activity lowering from the beta state (the level our brain is in when we are awake), to the alpha state (when we are dreaming and therefore closer to our subconscious). Alpha is the level at which you can tap into your psychic powers and project your spells.

2. Creating a pentacle circle of protection

Once you have reached this level, you need to create a pentacle circle of protection around your sacred area. The purpose of this is to enable you safely to achieve your mental projections without interference from negative, unbalancing, inappropriate energies and forces.

To create your circle, you need to imagine that the divine powers have sent you a ray of silver light. This light is so bright and electrifying that you reach out with both hands and grasp it. The energy of the light will travel down from your fingertips to the palms of your hands and thence to the rest of your body. Next, envisage a bright silver circle forming around you. This circle should include your altar. Then, through your mind's eye (sometimes called the third eye, behind the middle of your forehead), create an imaginary pentacle at each of the four geographical directions around your altar.

3. Purifying the pentacle circle of protection

Now that you have created the safety net around your sacred area, you must invite healing energies to purify your circle. This can be achieved by imagining a second beam of light, which is bright blue. It will fill up the inside of your circle, so that it has the effect of enveloping you. It should make you feel extremely relaxed and secure. Imagine all unsuitable energies being washed away.

Spend as long as you like adjusting to your circle. It should make you feel totally calm and confident in your own strength.

Once you feel ready for the task ahead, take a deep breath and slowly release it. Repeat this a few times.

Now close your eyes, begin to look through your mind's eye and repeat out loud:

> *★I form this pentacle circle of protection
> in the name of the divine powers.
> I heal and cleanse my circle, so that it is
> free of harmful and incorrect forces.
> My circle is now ready and filled with
> suitable energies for my magical work.*

4. Casting your spell

Then cast your spell as I have shown you. Put all your mental strength and power into the outcome of the spell.

5. Releasing your spell

When you have completed your spell, open your pentacle circle of protection by repeating:

*By opening this circle, I have freed my spell so that it is successful.
So it shall be.*

Your spell is like an arrow that you have fired into the universe to land at the right point – and only the sacred powers know exactly where that is. Once your spell has been released, you should then prepare yourself to return once more to the beta level of consciousness.

6. Returning to reality

With the palms of your hands open, raise your arms up in the air. Imagine the silver light leaving your body. As it does so, lower your arms and run your hands over your chakra points (the power points of the mind and body) beginning at the top of your head and ending at your feet. Then push your hands away from your body. Whilst you are performing this healing act, repeat:

I have now given my mind, body and soul a safe healing clearance. I am totally healthy and happy.

Finally start counting up from one to fourteen until you reach beta level. Now that you are 'back on earth', spend a few minutes adjusting again.

You have now returned to this world after successfully casting your first spell. Once a spell has been released, it is important to remember never to doubt yourself or the outcome of the spell. To introduce a lack of faith in your own ability is to create a rod for your own back and will result in the weakening of your spell.

If you have followed my guidelines, you can be sure that your spells will triumph. The knowledge that you have accumulated, combined with the gift of faith and positivity, should give you a powerful boost. However, such a gift should always be used wisely and with discretion, for every good action is followed by a good reaction.

HOW TO CREATE AND EMPOWER
A MAGICAL TOOL

Before you attempt to do this, make sure that you have
thoroughly read the previous section about shifting consciousness.

Wash your chosen object (unless it is food) in sea salt and water.
This has the effect of eliminating previous energies. Create a
pentacle circle of protection and meditate yourself into alpha
level. While holding the object, spend a few minutes observing
its temperature. As the temperature rises from cold to hot, begin
to squeeze the object.

Then repeat:

> *I cleanse this object in every way,*
> *it is now ready for me to energize.*

By squeezing the object, you are energizing it with your
powers. When you feel at the height of your power, say:

> *I energize this object* [state your purpose]

and then finish in the same way as other spells:

> *So it shall be.*

spells for
HEALTH

Create a symbol of protection and healing and place it outside your home. This can be a pentagram (an upright, five-pointed star with a circle around it) or it may be from any culture that appeals to you, whether pagan, Buddhist or American Indian.

Invite the different powers of the elements to help you in healing rituals.

Invoke the element of Water to counteract destructive energies such as hatred, anger and resentment. Water rules over the throat and heart area of the body.

Invoke the element of Fire to raise energy and bring about transformation and improvements. Fire rules over the solar plexus and the naval area.

Invoke the element of Air (wind) to release mental anguish and restore the balance and power of the mind. Air has the ability to clear and cleanse. It rules over the pineal gland and the crown of the head.

Invoke the element of Earth to ground you and attract stability into your life. Earth will help you to mature and draw new interests that are more suitable for you. It rules over the spine and the feet.

Perform this ritual for strength and overall healing. Sit

on the top of a hill at sunrise and attune your mind to

the sun. As the sun begins to rise, savor the intensity of

its colours and power enveloping you. Your skin will feel

warm and cleansed. Ask for the power and strength of

the sun to reflect in you and to heal you mentally,

emotionally and physically.

To help you recover from illness, ensure you use white bedding. This neutral colour contains cleansing and healing properties that will encourage a speedy recovery. Once you are safely on the healing road you may wish to add bursts of bright colours to invigorate you.

This spell is for neutralizing ill health.

REMOVING ILLNESS SPELL

Essential ingredients

3 cloves of garlic

small amount of salt

MAGIC FORMULA

In a pentacle circle of protection, energize the cloves of garlic to remove the illness safely from your body.

Go outdoors, away from your home, and bury the cloves of garlic. Place the salt under your mattress and leave it there until you feel healthy again.

To alleviate aches and overall physical and emotional exhaustion, dim the lights in the room. Next, lie down on the floor with a cushion beneath your head and two cushions under your knees to elevate them. You should feel physically supported but you may need to adjust the cushions in order

to be completely comfortable. Then place the palms of your hands on your midriff and take a deep slow breath, feeling your diaphragm and stomach expand with oxygen. Hold your breath for three seconds, then exhale slowly through your nose until you have released all the air. Repeat this procedure five to ten times without interruption whilst envisaging the oxygen as a healing energy travelling through your body.

Crystals are powerful healers, especially if you direct their magnetic energies for either a specific purpose or general enhancement. The following

Aries   Aventurine, Citrine, Tiger's eye, Topaz, Diamond, Ruby.

Taurus Amethyst, Moonstone, Pearl, Green Tourmaline, Jade, Selenite.

Gemini Pink Tourmaline, Garnet, Moss Agate, Carnelian, Pink Calcite, Beryl.

Cancer Amber, Kunzite, Lapis Lazuli, Sapphire, Moonstone, Citrine.

Leo   Chrysolite, Moldavite, Herkimer Diamond, Clear Quartz, Rose Quartz, Aventurine.

Virgo Peridol, Rutilated Quartz, Yellow Citrine, Meteorite, Clear Quartz and Citrine.

is a list of the sun signs and their complementary crystals. You may wish to wear the crystals, charge them or use them as an aid in meditation.

Libra	Malachite, Purple Fluorite, Garnet, Sugalite, Amazonite, Rose Quartz.
Scorpio	Aqua–Aura, Rhodochrosite, Sodalite, Turquoise, Ruby, Black Obsidian.
Sagittarius	Moonstone, Ruby Crystal, Jacinth, Orange Calcite, Rhodorite, Clear Quartz.
Capricorn	Onyx, Black Diamond, Garnet, Ruby, Bloodstone, Jet.
Aquarius	Topaz, Flourite, Amethyst, Aquamarine, Garnet, Rhodochrosite.
Pisces	Blue quartz, Fire Opal, Aquamarine, Hematite, Smoky Quartz, Clear Quartz.

Take a masculine smoky quartz and place it on the

crown of your head. This area controls the pineal gland

and represents the whole body and higher self. Hold the

crystal until you feel it heating up, knowing that it is

absorbing the negativity. Begin circling it around the top

of your head, gradually lifting it off fully. This process

will literally lift your spirits.

Lie down comfortably and place an amethyst crystal on

your third eye, at the centre of your forehead. This is the

pituitary gland, which affects your five other senses.

Ensure you are not wearing shoes or restrictive clothing.

Cup the amethyst with your left hand and close your

eyes. Relax and clear your mind, and take deep breaths

through your diaphragm until the crystal becomes hot.

This meditation will dissolve tension headaches and help

you to focus on dealing with any problems.

Your thyroid gland can be found at the base of your throat.

By placing a lapis lazuli or blue agate on this area, it will

help lower your pulse rate. This should be reinforced with

deep exhalation to bring about calm and tranquillity to

your body and mind. It is particularly effective if you are

prone to panic attacks.

A malachite stone or emerald held over your heart chakra will balance and regulate your blood pressure. This will further stimulate the supply of blood to your heart and to other parts of your body.

The day after the full moon, start a detoxification

programme for your body. This is an excellent time to

begin fasting and re-hydrating the body by drinking fluids.

But ensure that you do not have any health problems that

it may aggravate. This is only meant for a short period.

This ritual will detoxify your body and leave you feeling on form.

BODY-CLEANSING SPELL

Essential ingredients

Grapefruit bath oil

Cypress bath oil

Ylang-ylang body oil

Melissa body oil

Geranium body oil

MAGIC FORMULA

When the moon is on the wane, energize all the ingredients to purify and uplift your body.

Take a hot bath and pour several drops of the grapefruit and cypress oils into the water.

Visualize all the toxins in your body being washed away and feel cleansed.

Once you have finished your bath, mix together the ylang-ylang, melissa and geranium body oils and apply them generously to your body. As you rub the oils into your skin you will feel invigorated and complete.

Once a week open all the windows in your home. This

will remove stagnant energy that may generate ill health,

negativity and general problems. During winter open only

one window on each floor of the house. This will fill your

home with fresh energy.

Anxiety is like a toxin for the body. In order to eliminate

it, simply embrace activities that give you pleasure as this

will counteract the negativity. Having fun is good for

the mind as well as the body and allows us to keep our

worries in proportion.

When there is a storm go outside and stand with your arms open and raised. Call upon the power of the wind to restore your energy and vitality.

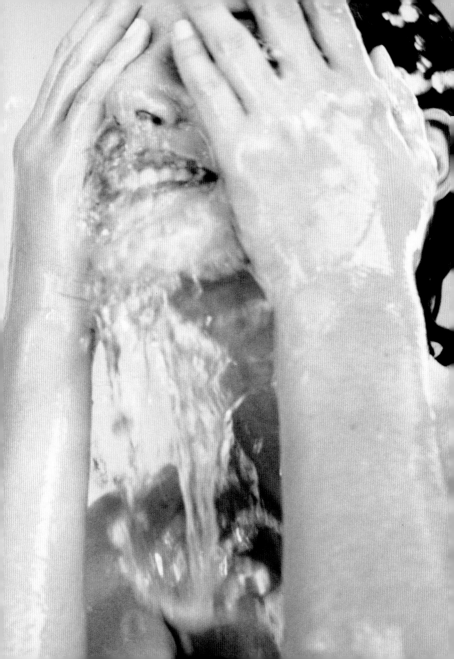

Place some eucalyptus leaves
in a bowl of warm water.
Leave them to soak overnight.
The next morning, remove
the leaves and wash your face
in the water. This infusion is
a natural deep cleanser and
has antiseptic properties.

Throw out or trim any dying or dead plants. This will help to promote and maintain good health in the home. Never keep dried flowers. Not only do they attract dust, which can aggravate asthmatic conditions and respiratory problems, but they also encourage negativity.

Light strawberry and frankincense incense sticks. Dedicate

them to cleansing your home and filling it with healing

and healthy energies. Then carry the incense in a

clockwise direction through each room in the house. As

the smoke leaves a trail through your home, visualize it

being a healthy place, free of negativity.

Drink valerian herbal tea in the early evening, especially

if you suffer from insomnia. This has a natural sedative effect and will help induce relaxation and sleep.

Place several drops of chamomile in an oil burner. Put the

burner in your bedroom and close the door. This will fill

the air with healing and relaxing energies and ensure a

deep sleep. When you go to bed, leave your door open to

allow good circulation.

This spell will bring you good health and good fortune.

54 GOOD HEALTH SPELL

Essential ingredients

Lemon teabag

Brown candle

Pink candle

MAGIC FORMULA

Energize the teabag with healthy energies.

Holding a candle in each hand, repeat:

*Good health and long life
blessed with good fortune.*

Then light the candles and repeat:

*I shall always have good health.
So it shall be.*

Leave the candles to burn down safely
and go and make a refreshing cup of
lemon tea. As you drink the tea, know
that your mind and body are in peak
condition.

spells for
WEALTH

To maintain a healthy nervous system, which is a necessary

ingredient of success, try including healthy brain foods,

such as avocados, rice, pulses and fruits, in your diet.

They nourish the mind and body and assist with

concentration.

Grow fresh mint and basil in your garden and the vicinity of your home. This will bring the necessary energies to acquire comfort and luxury. Replace any unhealthy herbs or plants, otherwise it can have the reverse effect.

Water is the element associated with wealth, money and emotions. Purchase a steady flowing water feature and place it in the north corner of your study.

To remove financial problems, begin this exercise on a Saturday night. Place seven cloves of garlic in a bowl and cover it with vinegar, then add three heaped tablespoons of sea salt. Next, using your index finger, stir the mixture clockwise. As you do so, visualize all your financial difficulties disappearing. Leave the bowl in your study overnight. The following day, bury the cloves in soil, away from your home and workplace. Throw out the vinegar.

A charming spell that will bring you material gains.

MAGICAL SHOES SPELL

Essential ingredients

Your favourite shoes

2 gold coins

2 drops of patchouli oil

MAGIC FORMULA

On the night of the new moon, go out into the garden.

Pour a drop of patchouli oil onto each coin.

Energize the coins to bring you material gain and place one coin in each shoe.

Put on the shoes, click your heels
together and repeat:

The spell has begun correctly.
So it shall be.

Keep the coins in your shoes until the
spell has begun to work.

Take two tablespoons of cloves, three tablespoons of

golden seal root and two tonka beans (available from

herbal shops). Crush the ingredients together in a pestle

and mortar, and visualize yourself being wealthy and

happy. Stir the mixture clockwise and then sprinkle it in

places where you store money such as a wallet, safe or cash

register.

Inscribe the rune symbol of Fehu in gold ink on a yellow or emerald green mug. Drink from it every morning to prompt gain and nourishment in your life.

Take a gold coin and cup it in between your hands. Now close your eyes and envisage wealth on all levels. Rub the coin against your stomach in a circular motion clockwise three times. Throw the coin into a stream.

Carry a gold, silver, or royal blue purse or wallet. The

colours are associated with attracting money. Never use an old or worn purse.

Line a deep blue bowl with red and silver silk fabric and keep your loose change in it. This will generate wealth, especially if you charge it with positive energy.

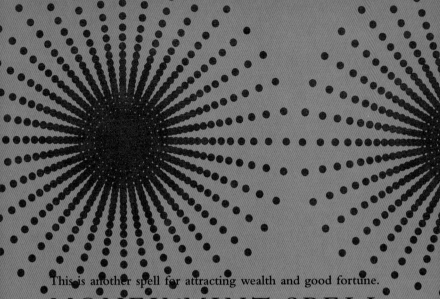

This is another spell for attracting wealth and good fortune.

MONEY MINT SPELL

Essential ingredients

Pestle and mortar

Sprinkle of mustard-seed powder

3 tablespoons spearmint powder

3 tablespoons red clover

3 tablespoons star anise

MAGIC FORMULA

Place all the ingredients in the mortar and pound them well.

Once the mixture is ready, energize it to bring you wealth and joy.

Then sprinkle the mixture into your bag or briefcase, or wherever you keep your wallet.

When there is a new moon dab a small amount of

peppermint oil onto a £50 or £20 note. Place it on a

window-sill in a secluded part of the house and cover it

with gold and silver coins. Look up to the sky and express

your wish for a raised standard of living. Ask for this to

come about appropriately and that it shall harm none.

Leave it overnight.

Take seven tablespoons of mustard seeds, one heaped

teaspoon of sandalwood powder and one drop of

heliotrope oil. Place the ingredients inside a navy blue

pouch and shake it well. Then squeeze the bag and repeat

'instant cash' several times. Carry it with you.

Use strong colours such as red, gold, orange and green in the northwest area of the home or at work to increase the influx of money.

Write on a small piece of gold, unlined paper the words:

great fortune, profit and riches

Then fold it and light a green candle. Drip the wax onto

one side of the paper and press a silver coin into it.

Repeat on the other side using another silver coin.

Place the paper, together with the attached coins,

underneath your mattress.

Take a gold coin and cup it in between your hands. Then close your eyes and envisage wealth on all levels. Rub the coin against your stomach in a clockwise circular motion three times.

Throw the coin into a stream.

Incorporate powerful colours and rich textures into your wardrobe to ensure money and good fortune.

Royal blue is ruled by the planet of Jupiter and attracts money and power.

Yellow and gold are ruled by the power of the sun and draw winning energies.

Silver is ruled by the power of the moon and influences successful people and also figures of authority.

Orange is ruled by Mercury and brings good fortune and good health.

Red is ruled by the planet Mars and is a powerful energizer.

Green is ruled by Venus and attracts fruition in business and professional growth.

This spell will bring you good luck and success.

LUCKY BOTTLE
SPELL

*Essential
ingredients*

Gold and blue bottle

Sandalwood chips

Bag of yellow mustard
seeds

Dried sunflowers

Yellow sand

Seashells

Pinch of salt

MAGIC FORMULA

Perform this ritual at dawn, before
sunrise.

Cleanse the bottle and fill it to the top
with all the ingredients.

Repeat:

*I create this magic bottle
to bring me luck and success
in all that I undertake.
So it shall be.*

Do not put the lid on the bottle. Release the spell and place the bottle in an area where you spend a great deal of time.

To enjoy a higher standard of living and a fulfilling career, burn red ginger and bergamot incense on a regular basis.

Keeping healthy plants and flowers in blue copper or gold pots on your desk at work will increase your chances of promotion.

This spell is for attracting money and influence.

COPPER CASH SPELL

MAGIC FORMULA

Essential ingredients

Copper bracelet

1 tablespoon myrrh powder

2 tablespoons basil

2 drops of frankincense oil

Pinch of salt

Small purple bag

Cleanse the bracelet and place the rest of the ingredients into the bag.

Shake the bag well, place the bracelet in the bag and recite the following words:

I cast a spell for money and influence to come my way, I wish to use them in a good way. So it shall be.

Wear the bracelet on your right wrist
and either carry the bag or leave it on
your desk at work.

A lodestone is a natural magnet for generating wealth and

attracting powerful and influential people into your life.

Whilst holding it in both hands, meditate for empowerment

and personal growth. Then wear it prominently.

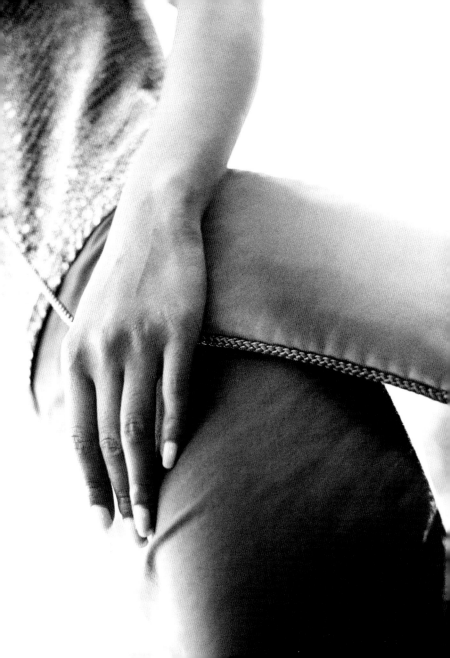

For important meetings or interviews, energize a

pointed blue or clear quartz crystal with winning

energies, and then discreetly wear it on a red or pink

ribbon around your neck.

For empowerment, light a
two-toned orange and gold
candle that is scented with
mint oil. Meditate on
increasing your drive and
self-confidence

Power bells are used for attracting and raising power energies. Place one in front of your filing cabinet or using silver cord, hang bells above it. This is for raising one's status in life.

Write the words 'expansion' and 'growth' on a green

ribbon and write your professional ambitions on a gold

ribbon. Plait them together and tie a knot at the end of

each ribbon. Then go outside, whether in the garden or

in the park, and tie the plaited ribbon to a branch of an

oak tree. Leave it there.

This simple spell will help you prosper and forge ahead in life.

PROSPERITY SPELL

*Essential
ingredients*

Quartz crystal

**33cm (13in) of blue
ribbon**

MAGIC FORMULA

Cast this spell on a day ruled by Jupiter, on or after the full moon.

Simply cleanse and energize the crystal to bring you prosperity and improvements in your life.

Hang the crystal from the ribbon and wear it around your neck for as long as you wish.

To keep you grounded, especially if you have a demanding job, carry a flat, smooth pebble. In times of pressure feel the texture of the stone in your hand and meditate on it. This has the ability to reassure you and give you a sense of calm.

The sea is a treasure of natural power. To make your

wishes come true, draw a circle in the sand, preferably

near the edge of the water, and add symbols of personal

happiness and good fortune. Give your wish to the sea

and then walk away.

Elemental meditation is very potent, especially for addressing specific problems in life.

In your bedroom form a large circle using pebbles. Then place a bowl of water, a round red candle and myrtle incense inside the circle. Then, whilst sitting in the circle, light the candle and incense and repeat:

> *Earth, Air, Fire and Water,*
> *I call upon your benevolent power to*
> *[name your objective].*
> *This shall happen correctly*
> *for the good of all.*

Meditate on the desired outcome for approximately twenty minutes, then extinguish the candle safely.

This ritual is very effective for making your hopes and dreams come true.

WISHING WHEAT SPELL

Essential ingredients

500g (18oz) of whole wheat

Small bowl

Small towel

Round tray

Tea towel

MAGIC FORMULA

On the day of the new moon, place the wheat in the bowl and cover it with water. Leave it to soak for three days but change the water daily.

After the three days, take out the wheat, place it in the small towel and tie it loosely. Leave it for another three days, occasionally spraying it with water.

On the third day, take out the wheat,
sprinkle it onto the tray and cover it
with the tea towel. Lightly spray the
wheat with water occasionally, so that
it stays moist.
Gradually you will notice that roots are
forming and that the wheat has begun
to sprout.

continued over...

Remove the tea towel, but continue to spray the wheat with water.

On the day of the full moon, take the tray to a river and cast a pentacle circle of protection. Whilst tying together a few strands of grass, repeat the following:

I tie these magic knots to bring about
the fulfilment of my wishes.
So it shall be.

Then remove all the wheat from the tray
and throw it into the river.

Walk away and do not look back because
your dream will come true.

spells for
HAPPINESS

Facing north, sit cross-legged with your elbows bent and

the palms of your hands held out towards the sky. Now

close your eyes and visualize two large balls of sunshine

weighing down your hands. As the balls become hotter

they will begin to feel lighter. Remain focused on this

imagery until you feel your palms rising upwards. See

the balls float up over your face and towards the top of

your head. As they pass they will warm you up. This

will instantly make you feel calmer and more positive.

Wear a turquoise or aquamarine ring on your sun finger, next to your index finger. This will draw harmonious and calming energies to the mind and spirit.

Polish the mirrors in your home so that they really shine – everyday dust can gather and accumulate negative energies. Keeping them clean will harness positive energies.

This spell will bring healing and happiness into your life.

HAPPINESS POTION

Essential ingredients

Iron pyrites (fool's gold)

Bornite (a mineral, copper or iron sulphide)

Sea salt

Water

MAGIC FORMULA

Perform this ritual on a Thursday when the moon is waxing.

Wash the pyrites and bornite in sea salt and water, then leave them upon a window-sill to dry naturally in the sun. Once dry, energize the mineral and the stone.

Then repeat out loud:

*I neutralize any negative energies, forces or
thoughts that may now be in me.
I charge them to bring happiness,
strength and healing into my life.
So it shall be.*

Once you have completed the process,
carry the pyrites and bornite on your
person for as long as required.

To uplift your spirits, add seven drops of helichrysum essential oil to a vaporizer. This will induce greater self-assurance and a higher sense of self-esteem.

To draw love and nourishment from the earth, sit on the

roots of a tree, or with your back against it. Taking some

quiet time out on your own allows you to reflect on your

true heart's desire.

If you seek emotional harmony and tranquillity in your life apply the following:

Create a circle of pink quartz, which is a master healer. Ensure the circle is big enough for you to stretch out in. Lie down with the palms of your hands flat on the ground and spread your fingers out. Even if it upsets you, slowly allow yourself to think about and feel your emotions. As you do so, tell yourself you are releasing your thoughts and feelings into the circle and you no longer hold onto negative emotions. You may feel like crying but that's okay. Once you feel you have released all those emotions that unbalance you, begin to sense the circle of crystals around you. They are radiating rays of healing energy and a sense of love into your mind and body. Visualize yourself floating on the powerful energy of the crystals. Take as long as you need. When you have finished, have a small snack to eat.

If you are a man, you can apply the same ritual, but you may wish to change the pink crystal to hematite as it is a more masculine stone.

For the more adventurous, under a full moon bathe

yourself in the sea whilst holding seven hematite stones.

Ask the sea to cleanse you of any negativity. Clear the

stones by washing them in sea salt and water, then

energize them to protect you correctly and to harm

none. If you are wary of swimming in the sea at night,

simply cleanse the stone at the edge of the water,

repeating the same ritual. Keep the stones close to you.

To rid yourself of a painful memory if possible wait till the dark of the moon, just before the new moon. Anoint one pink and one turquoise candle with lavender oil and light them. Then take a piece of white ribbon and project your pain into the ribbon as you tie seven knots into it.

Repeat:

> *I banish this pain immediately;*
> *I am healed in every way.*
> *This will happen correctly*
> *and it shall harm none.*

Use the turquoise candle to burn the ribbon but be careful not to hurt yourself.

This spell will cleanse your mind of a bad
dream that may have left you feeling anxious.

DREAM SPELL

*Essential
ingredients*

Water

MAGIC FORMULA

After a bad dream, go to the bathroom

sink and run the tap.

Wash your hands and face in the water

and repeat:

I cleanse my mind and body.
I neutralize any negative thoughts
and feelings.
I am refreshed.
So it shall be.

You will have erased the after-effects of
the bad dream.

Excessive arguing is not only unhealthy but it also has a

destructive element whereby it drains you of energy. Next

time you feel argumentative or as if someone is trying to

get a reaction out of you, make a real point of turning the

situation around. Light two silver candles and one pink

candle and some healing incense, such as orange blossom.

Focus on remaining calm and remind yourself how

destructive an argument can be. Shift your state of mind

by focusing on things that make you feel good.

If someone has upset you apply the following exercise. Make sure that you have no malicious intent when you are visualizing.

Sit in a quiet place and close your eyes. Begin to breathe slowly and deeply, then bring a clear image of the person who has upset you onto a screen in your mind. Next, start to encompass that person with white light until they have completely disappeared from your screen. Then, where their image appeared, replace it with a cool blue light. Repeat:

> *I am no longer hurt;*
> *they will not hurt me again.*
> *This is done correctly and shall harm none.*

Now open your eyes.

To encourage a reunion and heal a rift between friends that may have been blown out of all proportion, apply the following:

Pink shell stone

A fire opal

A copper bowl

4 tablespoons strawberry leaves

3 tablespoons of raspberry leaves

1 drop of jasmine essential oil

Whilst holding the stones in each hand, squeeze them and transfer your energy into the crystal. Close your eyes and visualize your friend's face. Forget about the fall-out and concentrate on envisaging a happy reunion. Don't try to manipulate who makes the first move, just allow yourself to be happy with the reconciliation. Next, place the stones in the bowl and cover them with the leaves and oil. Leave the bowl by your bedside at night, then the next day carry it with you until you see each other again.

This spell will help you to resolve your problems.

SOLVING A
PROBLEM SPELL

*Essential
ingredients*

Wood

Box of matches

Handful of esphand
(Persian ingredient
obtainable from
Eastern shops)

MAGIC FORMULA

Go outside and build a fire, taking care to
do so safely.

Sit in front of the fire and think carefully
about your problem. Once you have
worked out what, or who, is at the root
of your trouble, energize the esphand to
neutralize the problem.

Throw it into the fire and watch the
sparks fly out of it.

If you feel that you have been overwhelmed with problems

at work, try the following:

Take a bowl of warm water and mix in four tablespoons of

salt, one drop of lavender oil and one drop of frankincense

oil. Stir the ingredients together using a sprig of rosemary.

As you do so, visualize the problems being resolved.

Then sprinkle the mixture at each of the four corners of

your workplace.

Take up pottery to relieve tension. By getting your hands dirty, the clay will give you a sense of calm. Doing something creative and fun will further raise your sense of adventure.

To improve self-love and self-image, light seven pink candles for seven minutes at the same time for seven days. Focus solely on yourself and appreciate your worth.

To encourage harmony, go to a stream on a Wednesday

when the moon is waning. Put your hands in the water

and allow the natural movement of the stream to run the

water through your fingers. Feel the healing energies

washing away the discord in your life. Meditate on the

power of the water, the sound it makes as it passes by.

Visualize yourself being happy.

This spell will inspire you and reawaken your mind.

POSITIVE

INSPIRATION SPELL

*Essential
ingredients*

Oyster shell

Pink tourmaline

Four- or three-leaved
clover

Small silver magic bag

MAGIC FORMULA

At twelve o'clock on the night of the full
moon, place all the items in the bag and
squeeze it.

Cast the following spell:

Magic bag, magic bag,
*   filled with positive perception,*
*   awaken me so that I can have*
the benefit of your inspiration.
*   So it shall be.*

Release the spell and carry the bag with you.

Create a massage oil by adding one drop of chamomile roman to one teaspoon of sweet almond oil. Apply it to the skin. This will help to relieve worries and anxiety.

Fill a large bowl with boiling water and add four drops

of mandarin essential oil. As the steam begins to rise,

inhale the aroma slowly, being careful not to burn

yourself. To increase inhalation, you can hang a towel over

your head whilst you lean over the vapours. This will

boost your energy levels and stop you feeling negative.

Make a doll out of pink felt to represent you. Fill it up with hibiscus and myrrh. Personalize the doll. When the moon is on the wane, take the doll and hold it in both hands. Imagine that you are a greater and more powerful energy than your true physical self, bestowing strength onto the doll. To mend a broken heart, mark on the doll where the heart is and specifically send that area healing energies. You may project blue light upon it and then overall pink light for self-love. Repeat this until your pain has been replaced by your newfound resolve.

Lighting floating candles in water and meditating on them will encourage emotional balance. Incorporate different coloured candles to attract the following attributes:

Orange	*Overall love and strength*
Red	*Sex and passion*
Brown	*Family, children and home*
Blue	*Healing*
Gold	*Success*

During meditation, play music and ambient tunes to increase your chi (energy). Sit somewhere that inspires you and begin to focus your mind. Whilst listening to music, visualize the attainment of your goals. This should make you feel strong and confident.

Spend twenty minutes every day focusing on your goal.

Send healing loving energies to an absent partner.

Visualize their image and see them receiving your love

and being happy. Surround them with a warm pink light.

Spend approximately thirty minutes on this meditation.

This spell will boost your confidence and encourage you to love and trust yourself.

CONFIDENCE-
BOOSTING SPELL

Essential ingredients

9 silver candles

Large mirror

Lavender oil

Pink quartz crystal

MAGIC FORMULA

Arrange the candles to form a circle around yourself and the mirror.

Burn the lavender oil and cleanse the pink quartz crystal by washing it in water in which sea salt has been dissolved.

Cast a pentacle circle of protection and light all the candles.

As you are sitting in front of the mirror, stare at yourself and recite the following:

I love myself, I trust myself,
       I have confidence in myself.

Then energize the crystal and repeat the
above eight times.

When you have completed the spell, wear
the crystal close to your heart.

Leave the candles to burn down safely.

To help you move forward and leave the past behind, meditate using sugalite crystal. It is a stone of awareness and will take you into the future by opening your mind to the potential in life.

INDEX

INDEX

ACKNOWLEDGEMENTS

Getty Images: 2, 14, 20, 29, 38, 41, 46, 48, 63, 65, 78, 87, 99, 101, 102, 109, 121, 139
Photonica: 23, 31, 43, 55, 71, 80, 85, 93, 105, 115, 116, 117, 137
Photographers Library: 51, 129
Zefa: 56, 72, 97
All other images courtesy of Simon Wilde

Cover Image: Photonica

Designed by: Simon Wilder
Commissioning Editor: Camilla Stoddart
Editor: Robin Douglas-Withers